The
CABBAGE
Cookbook

by Ann L. Haslinger

Illustrations by Roland A. Moch

ARCO PUBLISHING COMPANY, INC.

New York

Published by Arco Publishing Company, Inc.
219 Park Avenue South, New York, N.Y. 10003

Copyright © 1974 by Ann Haslinger

Library of Congress Catalog Card Number 73-92076
ISBN 0-668-03442-4

Printed in the United States of America

Contents

An item taken from *The Monanch Dines,* by Theodore Hierneis, chef to King Ludwig II of Bavaria:

"In Fernstein, the king always ate Hectenkraut, a specialty which had often figured in royal menus during earlier reigns. This dish was prepared in the following way.

"A pike was baked and then allowed to get cold. All the bones were removed, even the very smallest, and the fish was cut up into small pieces and put on one side. Sauerkraut was then cooked with a lot of finely browned onions and plenty of butter. In a fireproof dish, greased with butter and lined with breadcrumbs, alternate layers of fish and sauerkraut were laid and the whole topped with breadcrumbs, covered with crayfish tails and the sauce and was browned for twenty minutes in the oven!"

This was the way of the kings! And cabbages are for kings.

Introduction

Cabbage is one of the most versatile of vegetables and blends with almost any spice or flavoring. It can be made sweet, sour, tart, bland, creamed, as a casserole, vegetable, dessert, salad, mold, relish, or as a part of a full one-dish meal.

A head of cabbage can always be kept on hand and used in any quick dish. To preserve it, the cabbage should be free of wilted leaves and kept in a cool refrigerator. If sealed, it will retain its nutritional value for many days. If a head of cabbage has been cut, always place the remainder in an air-tight container to keep it fresh until needed again.

Before you start to cook cabbage, be sure of your family needs. It cooks down to about one half of the original measure. Since it needs very little cooking, I recommend 10 minutes for the recipes that call for boiling cabbage, about 15 minutes for any sautéeing, and an hour or more for baking at 350°. Cabbage should be crisp and tender, and never overcooked, because it loses its texture.

I am not very heavy with spices so that all recipes call for only the minimal amount needed. Remember that spices tend to get stronger the next day, so experiment to your heart's delight. You can always add more spice at serving time, but you cannot take it out.

Sauerkraut, in any form purchased, is ready to eat. Some cooks like to drain and wash, while others like it with the sour juices. This is an individual taste. It can take more cooking than cabbage and makes up beautifully in many recipes.

For the cook seeking a low-calorie meal, cabbage can be used frequently. The only substitute you would make would be in the use of margarine instead of butter for the sauces. Use as little as possible and add the butter flavor in place of the butter.

Cabbage includes many varieties, such as white cabbage, winter cabbage, red cabbage, mild-flavored savoy, Brussels sprouts, and cabbage turned to sauerkraut.

Before the days of refrigeration, cabbage was the vegetable of kings because vitamin C was needed during the long winter months when garden fresh vegetables were not available. It is still a mainstay of the European diet. It is low in calories (only 30 calories per serving) but rich in vitamins A, B_1, B_2, Vitamin C, Vitamin K, calcium, phosphorus, iron, and other trace minerals needed for our bodies.

Several sauces can be made to compliment cabbage. Just as Southern cooking in America frequently uses beans, greens, and corn bread, others make a meal of cabbage mixed with other vegetables, meats, and a good thick rye or pumpernickel bread.

Even the inner core of the cabbage makes a tart accompaniment as a salad. Slice the core very fine and toss it with a dressing. It tastes like a radish or a turnip.

The following list describes the many spices and herbs that can enhance cabbage recipes. Start with one gentle shake to a portion and increase the amount as you like.

SUGAR AND SPICE; EVERYTHING NICE
BLENDS WITH CABBAGE

Allspice: Dried berry of the pimiento or allspice tree. It is aromatic, pungent, and compares in flavor to a cinnamon, nutmeg, and clove mixture.

Aniseed: Seeds of anise plant and member of the carrot family has a sweet smell with the flavor of licorice. Blends beautifully in any recipe calling for sweetened mayonnaise or honey.

Basil: Has a sweet and pungent aroma and taste.

Bay Leaf: Mild flavor from the laurel tree.

Capers: Grow in the Mediterranean sun with a flavor loved by French, Spanish, Italian, and Grecian cooks. They are usually pickled and have a tart flavor.

Caraway: These seeds are fragrant with a strong flavor and aroma. If fresh the flavor is tart and minty.

Cardamom: Has a mild, exotic flavor which is very aromatic. Frequently used in curries. Dried seeds can be used as a breath sweetener.

Cayenne: Has the fiery flavor of the small, hot red peppers. Adds zest and piquancy. Use sparingly.

Celery Seed: Imparts the flavor of celery without the bulk.

Chili: It is made from the ground pods of several Mexican peppers. Blended together it can include oregano, salt, cumin, and garlic.

Chives: A member of the onion family, is milder in taste. Can be used in place of scallions. Add the last minutes of cooking.

Cinnamon: Aromatic sweet flavor from the bark of the cinnamon tree.

Cloves: Most fragrant spice and resembles the nail head. It is usually ground to blend into cooking. Has an exquisite scent. Use sparingly.

Coriander: This pungent aromatic seed slightly resembles oregano and can be used to enhance the flavors of dishes using chili or needing extra zest.

Cumin: Has a light and spicy flavor. Used in Italian and Mexican cuisine.

Curry: A blend of spices from the East Indies or India. Many good curries have a blend of ten spices or more.

Dill: Seeds have a strong flavor somewhat like a caraway-mint mixture.

Fennel: Long used in French and Italian cooking, the entire plant is edible. Has a faint sweetish flavor like licorice.

Garlic: This ancient flavor is both loved and disliked. It is strong, spicy, and tasty, but also odorous for many hours. Used very extensively despite its odorous quality.

Ginger: Spicy, zesty flavor. Use sparingly as too much will make a dish taste bitter.

Horseradish: This root plant grows wild and has a delightful tangy, fiery taste, much sharper than onions or radishes.

Juniper Berries: Many times used to impart a bitter flavor. Can be substituted for gin in a recipe.

Leek: Strong taste of onion and garlic mixture. Very tasty but has some of the odorous qualities of garlic.

Mace: Mild and fragrant, can be used to substitute for nutmeg.

Marjoram: Belongs to the mint family but has a slightly bitter taste. Can be substituted for mint leaves.

Mint: Best known as a jelly with lamb. It is aromatic and cool tasting.

Mustard: This can be used dry or in its paste form. Has a lasting sharp, spicy flavor. Can be very hot or mild.

Nutmeg: This sweetish, spicy flavor has a seductive aroma. Use sparingly.

Onion: Common worldwide. This is the most commonly used of all flavors. It can impart a subtle flavor or a very strong flavor, depending on the varieties and amounts used.

Oregano: Loved by Mexican, Spanish, Italian, and Greek cooks it has a pungent flavor, similar to coriander. Some commerical oregano products have blends of mixed spices.

Paprika: True paprika comes from ground sweet red peppers. The imported paprika is hotter and more aromatic. Imparts a mysterious flavor.

Parsley: Can be hot or minty and tastes a bit like radishes. Beautiful as a garnish. Good raw and will counteract odors.

Pepper: A hot, spicy flavor that comes both black or white. It comes from the same tree but white pepper has had the outer coating of the seed removed before grinding. A very commonly known spice.

Poppy Seeds: Seeds come from the poppy plant and taste a bit like walnut with a licorice or anise flavor.

Rosemary: Smells like pine, very fragrant and does come from an evergreen shrub.

Saffron: Used to impart a yellow color and mild flavor to Italian, southern French, or Spanish cooking.

Sage: Has some of the flavor of the mint family. Has a musky, bitter flavor and must be used sparingly.

Scallions: These are the green tops of the small young onions. Chopped fine, they garnish and enhance the taste of raw salads. Cooked scallions impart the taste of cooked onions.

Sesame: These seeds have a nut-like fragrance and flavor. They blend well in salads.

Shallots: A member of the onion family, they have a milder flavor and aroma with the traits of a garlic-onion combination.

Sugar: Sweetener best known to all the world.

Thyme: Sparingly used, it adds a pungent taste. Add during the last few minutes of cooking.

Tumeric: Rich and peppery in taste, related to the ginger family. Use sparingly.

Vanilla: It has a sweet, strong taste. The richest kind comes from Mexico.

Watercress: This leafy plant has a peppery flavor and is best if you can find it fresh. Blends beautifully with raw cabbage to impart a pungent flavor; may resemble tart radish if very fresh.

Cabbage as a Vegetable

CABBAGE-CAULIFLOWER ALMONDINE

2 cups cut-up cabbage
2 cups cauliflower pieces
1 can cream celery soup
2 tablespoons butter
2 tablespoons slivered almonds
1 can of french fried onions

Place the cut up cabbage and cauliflower pieces in a greased casserole. Dilute the celery soup with a little water and pour over the cabbage and cauliflower. Melt the butter in pan and fry the almonds for 2 minutes. Mix the almonds with the french fried onions. Sprinkle over the casserole, cover, and bake 30 minutes at 350°. Serves 4–6.

SWEET-AND-SOUR CABBAGE WITH APPLES

1 medium head red cabbage, shredded
1 onion, minced
2 apples, peeled and diced
2 tablespoons oil
½ cup hot water
½ cup Burgundy wine
2 tablespoons brown sugar
2 tablespoons lemon juice
1 teaspoon salt
½ teaspoon pepper

Mix shredded cabbage, onion, and apple. Sauté in oil for 5 minutes. Add hot water and simmer 5 minutes more. Mix wine, sugar, lemon juice, salt, and pepper. Stir into cabbage and serve. Serves 6–8.

CABBAGE AU GRATIN

  4 cups cabbage, boiled
½ cup butter
  3 tablespoons flour
  1 teaspoon salt
½ teaspoon pepper
  2 cups milk
  1 tablespoon Worcestershire Sauce
½ cup cabbage stock
  2 cups bread crumbs
  1 cup grated American cheese

Cook the cabbage for about 15 minutes and save the stock. Melt the butter, add the dry ingredients, and mix thoroughly. Add the milk slowly, stirring constantly, and cook until thickened, about 2 minutes. Add the cabbage, Worcestershire sauce, and ½ cup of the cabbage stock. Turn into a buttered casserole dish. Sprinkle with the bread crumbs mixed with the grated cheese. Bake in oven at 350° for 20 minutes or until hot and browned. Serves 8.

10

CABBAGE IN BREMEN SAUCE

4 cups cabbage, shredded
1 teaspoon salt
2 tablespoons margarine
2 tablespoons flour
Pepper

Cook cabbage in salted water for about 10 minutes. Add the margarine. In a hot skillet, brown the flour, turning frequently. When it has turned brown, mix with enough cold water to make a paste. Pour into the cabbage and boil until slightly thickened. Season with pepper and serve.

CABBAGE IN WHITE CREAM SAUCE

2 quarts shredded cabbage
4 tablespoons margarine or butter
4 tablespoons flour
Water from the cooked cabbage
1 cup cream
Salt
Pepper
Chives or scallions

Shred cabbage until you have about two quarts. Place in a 3 quart pan, add water to cover and let it cook about 10 minutes. In a shallow pan, allow the margarine or butter to melt. Add the flour until you have a good paste. Drain some of the vegetable stock from the cooked cabbage and stir into the butter-flour mixture until the sauce is thinner. Add the cream, salt, pepper, and chives. Pour this cream mixture over the shredded cabbage. Heat immediately before serving. Serves 6–8.

CABBAGE IN CREAM CHEESE SAUCE

  4 cups shredded cabbage
  3 ounces cream cheese or 4 ounces cottage cheese
  ½ teaspoon salt
  ¼ teaspoon pepper
  ¼ teaspoon celery seed

Cook cabbage with one cup of water in a covered saucepan. Simmer for 10 minutes. Break cheese into small pieces and let it melt in the stock. Add seasoning. Serve hot. Serves 4.

EASY FRIED CABBAGE

1 onion, chopped
3 tablespoons oil or bacon drippings
4 cups shredded cabbage
Salt
Pepper
Sugar
Nutmeg
Vinegar

Heat pan and sauté onions in bacon drippings for 3 minutes. Add cabbage and sauté for 5 minutes, stirring frequently. Cover and allow to steam for 5 minutes. Use spices as desired from above list. Four cups of raw cabbage will serve 4.

HOT SLAW IN CASSEROLE
(Indian)

1 onion, shredded or diced
2 tablespoons butter
2 teaspoons flour
2 teaspoons curry
1 cup water
1 bouillon cube
½ clove garlic, grated
1 cup sour cream
¼ teaspoon pepper
¼ teaspoon ground cloves
4 cups shredded cabbage

Sauté the onion in butter. Mix in flour and curry powder. Add water, bouillon, garlic, and sour cream. Simmer until it thickens. Add remaining spices; simmer about 5 minutes. Place cabbage in a buttered casserole dish and pour sauce over cabbage. Mix well and bake at 350° for 20 minutes. Serves 4. Good with roast lamb.

CABBAGE AND MASHED POTATO
COLCANNON (Irish)

3 cups cooked cabbage, shredded
3 cups hot mashed potatoes
Salt
Pepper
Butter

Mix the cooked cabbage with the mashed potatoes and spices desired. Mix in butter to taste. (Instant potatoes can be used.)

CABBAGE NOODLE BAKE

¼ pound bacon, fried crisp
5 ounces noodles, uncooked
½ tablespoon sugar
1 teaspoon salt
4 cups shredded cabbage
½ teaspoon pepper
1 cup sour cream
½ teaspoon paprika

Fry bacon until crisp, drain, and set aside. Cook noodles until half done. Mix sugar and salt into bacon drippings in pan. Add cabbage and stir until coated. Cook over medium heat for 8 to 10 minutes, stirring continuously. Add the pepper and mix well. Combine cabbage, cooked noodles, and bacon in a greased casserole. Cover and bake at 350° for 20 minutes. Spoon the sour cream over the top, sprinkle with paprika, and bake another 10 minutes. Serves 6–8.

14

CABBAGE WITH RICE
(Greek)

½ pound bacon
1 large onion, chopped
1 can mushrooms (4 oz.)
4 cups shredded cabbage
1 cup rice
1 can tomatoes
½ cup raisins
1 cup bouillon
1 tablespoon honey
1 teaspoon lemon juice
Salt
Pepper
Nutmeg
Thyme
⅛ teaspoon garlic powder
White grapes for garnish

Fry bacon until crisp. Add onions and mushrooms. Sauté for 5 minutes. Mix all ingredients together and place in casserole. Cover and bake 1 hour at 250°. Add white grapes just before serving. Serves 6.

15

PIONEER CABBAGE

1 medium cabbage
2 eggs
½ cup cream
1 teaspoon salt
½ teaspoon pepper
Paprika
2 tablespoons butter

Chop cabbage in large pieces. Cover with hot water and simmer about 12 minutes. Drain and put into a casserole dish. Beat eggs and add cream, salt, and pepper. Pour over the cabbage. Sprinkle on the paprika and dot the butter evenly over top of the casserole. Bake at 350° for 30 minutes. Serves 6–8.

CABBAGE ON OUTDOOR GRILL

1 head cabbage, cut in wedges
Butter
1 pint prepared Bar-B-Que sauce
1 onion, sliced

Cut cabbage head into individual-size wedges. Place on heavy aluminum foil. Slice onion over wedges. Dot with butter, pour some Bar-B-Que sauce over each wedge and wrap in the aluminum foil. Grill on outdoor grill for about 30 minutes. Allow one wedge per portion.

CABBAGE WITH SOUR CREAM SAUCE

     2 cups red cabbage
     2 cups green cabbage (savoy can be used)
     1 tablespoon vinegar
     ½ stick margarine
     4 tablespoons flour
     1 teaspoon salt
     2 cups sour cream
     1 bouillon cube
Tabasco sauce to taste

   Cut cabbage into small wedges. Cook in covered pan with water and vinegar. Simmer for 10 to 12 minutes. Add margarine to water. Mix flour with a little water. Slowly add to the cabbage, mixing to keep smooth. Add the salt, sour cream, bouillon cube, and Tabasco sauce. Serve hot. Serves 6.

TEXACANO CABBAGE

   1 head cabbage, coarsely chopped
   1 tablespoon sugar
   2 tablespoons butter
   1 onion, sliced
   1 green pepper, diced
   2 cups canned tomatoes
   1 teaspoon salt
   ½ teaspoon ground cumin
   ½ teaspoon chili powder
   ¾ cup shredded Cheddar cheese

   Simmer cabbage in a saucepan with a little water until tender, about 10 minutes. Drain and put in a buttered two-quart saucepan or casserole. Sauté the sugar, butter, onions, and green pepper in a saucepan. Add the tomatoes and spices. Pour the mixture over the cabbage in the casserole, sprinkle the shredded cheese over the top and bake at 350° for 30 minutes. Serves 8.

RED CABBAGE PIQUANT

½ cup diced bacon
4 cups red cabbage, shredded
½ cup diced onion
2 cups diced apple
1 teaspoon salt
½ teaspoon pepper
2 tablespoons vinegar
1 teaspoon cinnamon
½ teaspoon nutmeg
¼ teaspoon ginger

Brown the bacon and set aside. Place cabbage, onions, and apples in a heavy skillet. Toss and cover. Cook over low heat for 10 minutes. Add all other ingredients. Simmer 5 minutes longer and serve. Serves 6–8.

RED CABBAGE WITH WINE

  1 large onion, minced
Cooking fat
  1 medium head red cabbage (2 quarts shredded)
  2 tablespoons cornstarch
  1 teaspoon salt
¼ teaspoon pepper
¼ cup honey or sorghum
¼ cup vinegar
½ cup red wine
  1 apple, diced
  1 cup apple jelly

Sauté onion in fat until slightly brown. Add the cabbage to the onion. Mix cornstarch in ¼ cup cold water. Add all other ingredients and pour over cabbage, stirring until sauce has thickened. Cook about 20 minutes until cabbage is soft but still crisp. Serves 8.

LEFTOVERS AND CABBAGE VARIATIONS

I: 1 quart cooked cabbage
1 pint cooked white beans
Spices

Heat together and serve.

II: 1 quart cooked cabbage
1 cup raw oatmeal
Spices
Dash vinegar

Heat together and serve.

III: 1 quart cooked cabbage
1 pint cooked split green peas
Spices

Heat together and serve.

IV: 1 quart cooked cabbage
1 cup mushrooms
1 onion, minced

Sauté mushrooms and onions in margarine. Add to cabbage. Heat.

21

V: 1 quart cooked cabbage
1 quart mashed potatoes
Spices

Heat together and serve.

VI: 1 quart cooked cabbage
1 cup tomatoes
1 cup rice

Heat together; add spices as desired.

VII: 1 quart cooked cabbage
2 cups noodles
1 minced onion
Margarine

Sauté together; season.

Cabbage with Meats

CABBAGE WITH WATER CHESTNUTS AND MEAT

4 cups chopped cabbage
4 tablespoons oil
1 crushed garlic clove
1 cup sliced, cooked water chestnuts
2–3 cups cooked meat such as beef, pork, lamb, tongue, knockwurst, Polish sausage, or poultry
1 cup rice

Sauce:
  3 tablespoons margarine
  2 tablespoons cornstarch
  2 cups vegetable stock
  ½ teaspoon ginger
  3 tablespoons soy sauce
  ½ cup chopped scallions
  2 tablespoons minced parsley

Cooked chopped cabbage in boiling salted water for 10 minutes. Strain and save stock. Add oil, crushed garlic, water chestnuts, and beef to cabbage. Cook 1 cup of rice according to package directions. Set aside and keep warm.

In the top of a double boiler, over simmering water, melt the margarine. Mix in the cornstarch and slowly add the vegetable stock. Stir constantly until the sauce has thickened and is smooth. Add all other ingredients. Pour the sauce over the cabbage mixture and heat thoroughly. Serve over cooked rice. More soy sauce may be added at the table. Serves 6.

CORNED BEEF AND CABBAGE

3–4 pounds brisket of corned beef
1 bay leaf
Peppercorns
4 onions
6–8 peeled potatoes
6–8 peeled carrots
1 head cabbage, cut in wedges
Hot mustard
Horseradish

Cook the corned beef, covered with water, in a large covered pot with bay leaf and peppercorns. Keep on low heat for about 3 hours or until meat is just tender. Drain off the water and remove the peppercorns and bay leaf. Add fresh water to the pot, put in the carrots, potatoes, and onions. Cook 15 minutes then add the cabbage wedges. Cook 15 to 20 minutes longer. Add salt and pepper if needed (this depends on the curing of the corned beef). Remove corned beef and slice. Serve on a large platter with the vegetables surrounding the meat. Use horseradish and hot mustard as desired. Serves 6–8.

QUICK CORNED BEEF AND CABBAGE IN CASSEROLE

3 cups cooked cabbage
1 can whole potatoes (1 pound size) or fresh boiled
    potatoes
1 can corned beef, sliced
1 onion, sliced
½ cup shredded Cheddar (or American) cheese
1 can condensed soup, such as celery or mushroom
1 tablespoon dry mustard
1 tablespoon steak sauce
1 soup can water

Place a layer of cooked cabbage on the bottom of a buttered casserole. Arrange a layer of small potatoes, sliced corned beef, and sliced onions. Alternate layers according to the size of the casserole. Sprinkle the shredded cheese over top. Mix the canned soup with the dry mustard, steak sauce, and water. Pour over the casserole. Bread crumbs can be used to top the casserole. Bake at 350° for 25 to 30 minutes. **Serves 3–4.**

BEEF WITH CABBAGE IN CASSEROLE

  1 medium head cabbage, diced
  1 pound lean ground beef
  1 cup uncooked rice
  1 teaspoon salt
 ½ teaspoon pepper
  1 teaspoon chili powder
 ¼ teaspoon cumin
 ¼ teaspoon Tabasco sauce
 ½ teaspoon onion powder
 ¼ teaspoon garlic powder
  1 cup tomato sauce
 ½ cup water

Mix diced cabbage with ground beef and rice and put in a greased casserole. Mix all other ingredients together and pour over the top. Bake at 350° for 45 minutes or until rice is tender. Serves 8 or more.

28

FRANKFURTERS WITH CABBAGE IN CASSEROLE
(Sweet-and-Sour Sauce)

4 cups shredded cabbage
8–10 frankfurters
3 tart apples, cored and sliced
1 onion, sliced
Margarine
1 cup bread crumbs

Sweet-and-Sour Sauce:
½ stick margarine
½ cup brown sugar
1 cup water
¼ cup vinegar
½ teaspoon salt
2 tablespoons cornstarch
½ cup jelly—apricot, apple, or peach

Cook cabbage in a covered saucepan in salted water for about 8 minutes. Drain and place a layer of cabbage on the bottom of a buttered casserole. For the second layer, use cut-up frankfurters, apple slices, and the onion slices. Alternate layers until all ingredients are used. Dot with butter.

Make the sauce by melting the margarine in a saucepan and stirring in all other ingredients. (Mix cornstarch in cold water before adding to the saucepan.) Pour sauce over the cabbage, top with the bread crumbs, and bake at 350° for 25 to 30 minutes. Serves 6–8.

HAM AND CABBAGE IN CASSEROLE

    4 cups cabbage, cut coarsely
    3 cups diced ham
    ½ cup minced onion
    1 stick margarine
    4 tablespoons flour
    2 cups milk
    1 cup grated Cheddar or American cheese
    1 teaspoon celery seed
    1 teaspoon salt
    1 teaspoon pepper
    1 cup buttered bread crumbs

Sauté the ham, onion, and cabbage in a little margarine until the cabbage is slightly wilted. Melt ½ stick of margarine in the top of a double boiler over simmering water. Mix in the flour and slowly add the milk and cook, stirring, until the sauce is smooth and thickened. Add the cheese, celery seed, salt, and pepper, and stir until the cheese melts. Place the ham and cabbage mixture in a casserole. Pour the sauce over, dot with the remaining margarine and top with bread crumbs. Bake for 30 minutes at 350°. Serves 6–8.

SAVORY HAM AND CABBAGE SALAD
(Complete Meal)

3 medium tomatoes
2 cups cooked peas
½ cup diced celery
Black olives
3 cups shredded cabbage
1 cucumber, sliced
2 hard cooked eggs, sliced
2 cups ham, diced or sliced
1 cup mayonnaise
1 cup sour cream
½ cup chive tops
½ tablespoon horseradish
½ teaspoon salt
¼ teaspoon pepper

Mix mayonnaise with sour cream, chives, horseradish, and spices. Let it stand for several hours or overnight. Scoop the center out of the tomatoes and drain the shells. The center of the tomatoes may be mixed with the shredded cabbage. Toss peas, celery, and diced olives together. Moisten with dressing. For serving, line large salad bowl with shredded cabbage. Place tomato cups on cabbage and fill with salad mixture. Place a ring of the egg, ham, and cucumber slices around each tomato cup. Top with more dressing. Serves 6.

CABBAGE-HAM
(Quick Meal Casserole)

1 medium cabbage, shredded
2 cups diced ham
Salt
Pepper
1 can cream of mushroom soup
1 soup can of water
½ cup grated Cheddar cheese
½ cup bread crumbs

Cook cabbage in water for about 10 minutes (pre-cooked cabbage can be used). Mix cabbage with ham. Season to taste and put in buttered casserole. Mix soup with water and pour over the cabbage mixture. Top with crumbs. Bake uncovered at 350° for 30 minutes. Serves 6–8.

STEW WITH HAM AND CABBAGE
(Cooked Version)

8 carrots
Salt
Pepper
8 medium potatoes
8 medium onions
1 head cabbage, cut in 8 wedges
1 canned ham (3 pounds) or any smoked meat, such as
    frankfurters or corned beef
Mustard
Horseradish

Place whole carrots in a saucepan with about 2 inches of water. Season with salt and pepper. Boil for 10 minutes. Add the potatoes and onions. Boil for another 10 minutes. Add the cabbage and the canned ham. Cook for 12 to 15 minutes more. Serve with mustard or horseradish along and dark bread. Serves 8.

STEW WITH HAM AND CABBAGE
(Quick Version)

1 can carrots
1 can onions
1 can small potatoes
1 pound franks or canned ham
1 head cabbage in wedges

Place all ingredients (including the juices from the canned vegetables) in a large saucepan and cook only until the cabbage is soft, usually about 15 minutes. Spice as desired. Serves 6–8.

KNOCKWURST WITH APPLES

1 small head cabbage cut in 6 sections
1 cup chopped apples
1 can condensed cream of celery soup
1 can milk
1 teaspoon caraway seed
1 teaspoon aniseed
6 knockwurst

Cook cabbage in saucepan with a little water for about 5 minutes. Drain. In shallow baking dish combine the cabbage and apples. Mix the soup with the spices and pour over the top. Place knockwurst on top. Bake at 350° for 35–40 minutes. Serves 6.

PIG HOCKS WITH WHITE CABBAGE

3–4 pounds pig hocks
Salt
1 large head cabbage, cut in 8 wedges
Pepper
Boiled potatoes
Horseradish

Simmer the pig hocks in salted water for 3 hours. Add the cabbage and pepper and cook for another 30 minutes. Boil the potatoes in a separate pan. Place the pig hocks on a large platter surrounded by a ring of potatoes and cabbage wedges. Dot horseradish over the pig hocks. Hot rye bread or rolls are served frequently with this dish. Serves 8.

LAMB WITH CABBAGE
(Norwegian or Scandinavian Dish)

4–5 pounds lamb, cut in 1½-inch pieces
Cabbage head, cut in 1-inch pieces
  1 cup diced celery
  2 teaspoons salt
  2 teaspoons pepper
½ cup flour
  2 cups bouillon
½ cup sour cream

In a large, heavy saucepan place a layer of lamb with the fatty side down. Cover with a layer of cabbage and sprinkle with diced celery, salt, pepper, and flour. Repeat the layers until all ingredients are used. (There are usually about three layers.) Add the bouillon about halfway up the saucepan. Cover with a tight lid and bring to a boil. Simmer for 2 to 2½-hours or until the lamb is tender. Add more bouillon if necessary. Just before serving, stir in the sour cream and mix thoroughly. Serve hot with boiled potatoes. Serves 6–8.

EXCITING PORK CHOPS WITH
CHESTNUTS AND CABBAGE

        8 pork chops
        1 pound sweet Italian sausage, cut in 1-inch pieces
        1 head red cabbage
      3–4 cooking apples, sliced
    16–18 roasted chestnuts
        3 onions, sliced
       ¼ cup fresh chopped parsley
       ½ teaspoon ground cloves
       ½ teaspoon cinnamon
        2 teaspoons salt
        1 teaspoon pepper
       ½ cup brown sugar
       ½ cup red wine or wine vinegar
Currant or apple jelly

Brown pork chops and sausage in a frying pan for 15 minutes. Place in a deep casserole. Top with the cabbage, apples, chestnuts, sliced onions, and parsley. Mix seasonings with the wine vinegar or red wine. Pour over the entire casserole and bake at 350°, covered, for 1 hour. Serve the jelly on the side or dropped on each serving. Serves 4.

SAUSAGE AND CABBAGE IN CASSEROLE

1 pound bulk sausage, hot or mild
1 medium cabbage, shredded
3 apples, diced
1 teaspoon salt
1 tablespoon vinegar
½ cup honey

Mold sausage into flat cakes and fry for 5 minutes until browned on both sides. Sausage links can be used. Put a layer of shredded cabbage in a casserole dish, top with a layer of apples and season with salt. Continue the layers until the cabbage and apples are all used. Place sausage on top. Mix vinegar with honey. Pour over cabbage. Cover casserole and bake 45 to 50 minutes at 350°. Serves 6–8.

SHORT RIBS WITH CABBAGE
(Francaise)

5 pounds short ribs
1 bay leaf
2 cloves
Sprig parsley
1 clove garlic
2 teaspoons salt
1 teaspoon pepper
4 carrots, cut in a half
1 turnip, cut in quarters or less
6 small onions
6 leeks, or wild onions
1 small head cabbage
1 rib celery, cut in small pieces
6 small potatoes
Grated fresh horseradish
Coarse salt

Place the short ribs in a large kettle, cover with enough water and bring to a boil. Simmer for 3 to 4 hours. Tie the garlic, bay leaf, cloves, and parsley in a cheese cloth bag and add to the meat. Add the spices and the vegetables. Boil until tender, about 35 minutes. Serve on a large platter; use horseradish and coarse salt for flavor and garnish. The soup can be saved for another meal to make a thick vegetable soup. Serves 5–6.

CABBAGE SUKIYAKI

1 stick butter
4 cups chopped cabbage
1 cup chopped onion
1 cup chopped green pepper
1 cup chopped celery
Salt
Pepper
3 cups finely sliced top round steak

Melt the butter in a very large skillet. Add the cabbage and sauté it for about 3 minutes, stirring often. Push the cabbage to one side and add the onion and sauté it for 3 minutes. Push the onion over near the cabbage and add the green pepper. Sauté the green pepper for 3 minutes, push it to the side and add the celery and sauté it for 3 minutes. Add salt and pepper to taste. Push the celery to the side and add the steak slices and sauté them until they are a rich brown. Serve immediately. Serves 4.

CABBAGE AND FISH CASSEROLE

1 head cabbage, cut in small wedges
1 can mackerel, salmon, or other canned fish
Margarine
½ cup sweet pickle relish
½ cup bread crumbs
1 teaspoon salt
½ teaspoon pepper

Boil cabbage wedges in salted water for about 10 minutes. Drain. In casserole mix the cabbage and mackerel. Dot with margarine. Mix the bread crumbs with the sweet relish, season with salt and pepper. Spread over top of casserole. Bake at 350° for 20 minutes. Serves 4–6.

HAM ROLLS WITH CABBAGE FILLING

2 cups cooked cabbage
Salt and pepper
10 slices boiled ham
3 tablespoons flour
2 cups milk
1 tablespoon margarine
1 teaspoon salt
½ teaspoon pepper
1 cup grated Cheddar cheese

Season the cooked cabbage. Place about 2 tablespoons on each ham slice. Roll the ham around the cabbage and place in a casserole dish. Mix the flour with milk; add the margarine, salt, pepper, and cheese. Boil until the sauce is blended. Pour over the ham rolls and bake for 20 minutes at 400°. Serve 2 per portion.

CABBAGE AND CRAB MEAT CASSEROLE

4 cups shredded cabbage (plain or Chinese)
3 tablespoons margarine or oil
8 ounces crab meat
1 tablespoon sherry
1 tablespoon cornstarch
1 cup stock or water
1 teaspoon salt
Margarine

Cut up cabbage and sauté in a little margarine only until wilted. Place in a casserole dish. If the crab meat is not cooked it should be sautéed in the same pan for 2 to 3 minutes. Add to the cabbage. Pour in the sherry. Mix the cornstarch with stock or plain water. Season with salt and stir until the sauce thickens and is smooth. Pour over casserole. Dot with margarine. Sprinkle bread crumbs on top and bake at 350° for 30 minutes. Serves 4–6.

Slaws, Salads, and Molds

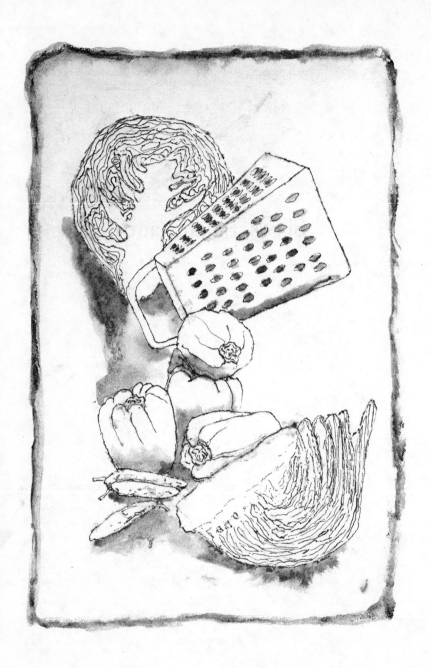

COLE SLAW WITH LOW CAL DRESSING

Slaw:

3 cups shredded cabbage
1 cup shredded carrot

Dressing #1:

½ cup herb vinegar
½ cup water
¼ teaspoon pepper
½ teaspoon salt
Low calorie sweetener to taste

Combine all ingredients.

Dressing #2:

½ cup sweet pickle juice
½ cup juice from sour pickle
½ teaspoon salt

Mix and let stand.

Dressing #3:

¼ cup low cal mayonnaise
¼ cup vinegar
¼ cup sweet relish

Mix together, blend well.

Dressing #4:

¼ cup low cal mayonnaise
¼ cup low cal sour cream
½ cup sweet pickle juice

Mix together well.

Dressing #5—French Dressing:

¼ cup vinegar
¼ cup chili sauce
1 teaspoon salt
¼ teaspoon pepper
½ teaspoon paprika
1 teaspoon sweetener (to taste)
1 tablespoon oil
Garlic clove, cut
½ cup pickle juice

Mix together, let stand 1 hour.

Dressing #6:

Low-Cal Sour Cream Dressing
½ cup buttermilk
1 cup low cal cottage cheese
¼ cup pickle juice
1 teaspoon lemon juice

Combine all in blender.

Dressing #7:

½ cup water
½ cup vinegar
1 teaspoon paprika
1 tablespoon Parmesan cheese
1 teaspoon Worcestershire sauce
½ teaspoon salt, some sweetener
½ teaspoon oregano flakes

Blend well; stir just before use.

Optional Add-On:

String beans, cooked
Peas, cooked
Beets, cooked
Cucumbers
Sweet or sour pickles
Relish
Tomato
Onion, sliced or diced
Horseradish
Celery
Chinese cabbage
Green pepper
Garlic, pressed or grated
Radishes

SLAW WITH COTTAGE CHEESE

¾ cup mayonnaise
3 tablespoons lemon juice
1 teaspoon onion powder
½ teaspoon salt
½ teaspoon pepper
1 cup cottage cheese
1 quart finely shredded cabbage
1 carrot, grated
1 apple, diced fine
Large lettuce leaves
Green pepper slices (optional)

Combine the mayonnaise, lemon juice, onion powder, salt, and pepper. Mix cottage cheese with cabbage, carrots, and apples. Pour dressing over mixture and let it stand for several hours. Place large lettuce leaves on a serving plate. Arrange slaw and cheese on the leaves. Garnish with green pepper slices. Serves 6.

SLAW WITH PEANUTS

4 cups shredded cabbage
1 cup shredded carrot
½ cups salted peanuts
½ teaspoon pepper
½ cup raisins
½ teaspoon aniseed
1 cup mayonnaise

Combine all ingredients, coating well with mayonnaise or salad dressing. Serves 6–8.

HOT CABBAGESLAW

1 large onion, sliced
3 tablespoons butter
1 head cabbage, shredded
½ cup honey
1 teaspoon salt
½ cup wine vinegar
½ cup water
½ teaspoon cinnamon
¼ teaspoon ginger
1 tablespoon dry mustard
1 cup sour cream

Melt butter and sauté onion until soft. Add cabbage and cook for about 10 minutes. Combine water, vinegar, honey, and spices. Pour over cabbage and cook for another 5 minutes. Just before serving add the sour cream. Mix and serve hot. Serves 6–8.

MEDITERRANEAN SLAW

4 cups shredded cabbage
½ cup of chopped dates
½ cup mayonnaise
1 tablespoon prepared mustard
¼ cup honey
¼ cup sour cream

Mix cabbage with dates. Blend remaining ingredients well. Toss with the cabbage and allow to blend well for an hour or more. Serves 6.

CABBAGE AND PINTO BEAN SALAD

1 cup cooked cabbage
1 cup cooked pinto beans (canned)
1 tablespoon pimiento slices
2 tablespoons olive oil
2 tablespoon vinegar
1 teaspoon salt
½ teaspoon pepper

Combine the cabbage and the pinto beans. Add pimiento slices. Toss with a dressing made of vinegar, oil, salt, and pepper. Serves 4–6.

POLYNESIAN SLAW

4 cups shredded green cabbage
2 mandarin oranges, sliced
1 cup crushed pineapple, drained
½ teaspoon salt
½ cup mayonnaise
¼ teaspoon white pepper
¼ cup orange juice
½ cup pineapple juice
¼ teaspoon anise
¼ teaspoon ground ginger
¼ teaspoon nutmeg

Shred cabbage and mix with orange slices and drained pineapple. Mix all other ingredients to make a dressing and stir until smooth. Chill. Toss over cabbage mixture an hour or two before serving. Serve 6–8. Good with chicken or ham.

SWEET-'N-SOUR SLAW

½ cup ripe olives
½ cup green olives
 2 tablespoons sliced pimiento
 4 cups cabbage finely shredded
¾ cup mayonnaise
½ cup sour cream
¼ cup lemon juice
 1 teaspoon dry mustard
 1 teaspoon salt
½ teaspoon onion powder
½ teaspoon pepper
½ teaspoon celery seeds
½ teaspoon anise
 2 tablespoons brown sugar

Sliver olives fine, slice pimiento, and mix with the shredded cabbage. Mix all other ingredients together. Toss with the cabbage mixture and allow to stand several hours. Serves 8–10.

SOUTHERN COLE SLAW

1 head cabbage, cut as desired
1 carrot, diced fine
1 onion, diced very fine
½ cup hot bacon drippings
½ cup sugar
½ cup herb vinegar
½ teaspoon salt
¼ teaspoon pepper

Cover cabbage, carrot, and onion with water and place in refrigerator to become firm. Just before serving, heat the bacon drippings with the sugar, vinegar, salt, and pepper. Drain the cabbage well and pour over it just enough hot dressing to saturate it well. This will keep in the refrigerator for several days. Serves 10.

CABBAGE AND TOMATO SALAD

3 cups shredded cabbage
2 tomatoes, chopped
2 scallions, chopped
½ cup mayonnaise
½ teaspoon salt
2 tablespoons lemon juice

Combine cabbage, tomatoes, and scallions. Mix mayonnaise with lemon juice and salt. Toss with cabbage and serve. Serves 6.

TANGY MOLD OF FRESH VEGETABLES

  1 package lime gelatin
  1 cup boiling water
 ½ cup cold water
  1 tablespoon vinegar
 ¼ teaspoon salt
 ¼ teaspoon pepper
 ½ cup mayonnaise
 ½ cup shredded carrots
 ½ cup shredded cabbage
 ¼ cup sliced radishes
  1 tablespoon minced onion
Salad greens
Radishes
Sliced cucumbers

Pour the boiling water over the gelatin. Beat the mayonnaise with cold water, vinegar, salt, and pepper and add to the gelatin. Chill until thick, then beat with a beater until frothy. Stir the vegetables into the gelatin and allow to set. Invert on dish of salad greens; garnish with radishes and sliced cucumbers. Serves 8.

APPLESAUCE-CABBAGE MOLD

 1 package plain gelatin
½ cup apple juice
 2 cups applesauce
½ cup sugar
½ cup lemon juice
½ teaspoon salt
 1 tablespoon horseradish
 1 cup finely chopped cabbage
½ cup raisins
½ cup chopped celery
Lettuce leaves
½ cup shredded carrots
Mayonnaise or salad dressing

Soften gelatin in the apple juice. Heat the applesauce and add the softened gelatin; stir until dissolved. Add sugar, lemon juice, salt, and horseradish. Cool until slightly thickened. Mix in the cabbage, raisins, and celery. Pour into individual molds that have been rinsed in cold water. Allow the mixture to chill until well set. Just before serving unmold onto lettuce leaves and garnish with the mayonnaise and carrot shreds. This will make 6 portions.

54

COLE SLAW IN TOMATO ASPIC

  1 quart tomato juice (or V-8 Juice)
  2 packages plain gelatin
¼ cup lemon juice
  2 teaspoons dry sherry
Tabasco Sauce
½ teaspoon salt
  2 cups finely shredded, very green cabbage
Mayonnaise

Pour 1 cup of tomato juice over both packages of gelatin. Heat 1 cup of tomato juice and add to the gelatin mixture and stir until the gelatin is dissolved. Add the lemon juice, sherry, a dash of Tabasco, salt, 2 cups of cold tomato juice, and any other seasoning you might like. Pour the gelatin-tomato juice mixture into a large mold. Let it set until it starts to thicken. Add the shredded cabbage. When unmolded, garnish with mayonnaise or slaw dressing. Serves 8–10.

PINEAPPLE-CABBAGE MOLD

  2 packages pineapple flavored gelatin
3½ cups boiling water
  3 cups shredded cabbage
  1 cup chopped tart apples
 ½ cup diced canned pineapples, drained
  1 cup chopped celery
 ¼ cup lemon juice

Dressing:
½ cup mayonnaise
½ cup pineapple juice
Aniseed

Dissolve the gelatin in boiling water and stir well. Let it chill until it becomes like heavy syrup. Combine the shredded cabbage, apples, celery, and pineapple. Dribble over the lemon juice. Add to gelatin and chill it in large mold (2½ to 3 quarts). Serve with a dressing of mayonnaise, pineapple juice, and aniseed. Serves 10.

PERFECTION SALAD

    1 envelope plain gelatin
    ½ cup cold water
    1 cup boiling water
    2 tablespoons vinegar
    ¼ cup sugar
    ½ teaspoon salt
    1 teaspoon Worcestershire Sauce
    ¼ teaspoon allspice
    2 cups shredded cabbage
    1 cup diced celery
    ¼ cup sweet pickle relish
    ¼ cup broken olives
Lettuce leaves

   Soften gelatin in cold water. Let it stand 5 minutes then add boiling water and stir until gelatin dissolves completely. Add the vinegar, sugar, salt, Worcestershire Sauce, and allspice (or other spices as desired). Chill until slightly thickened. Mix all other ingredients and fold into gelatin. Pour into mold that has been slightly oiled or into 6 individual molds. Chill for 4 hours before serving. Unmold on lettuce leaves.

Soups and Sandwiches

CHICKEN POT-AU-FEU

Step I:
1 (3 pound) chicken, cut up
1 onion
2 stalks celery
1 carrot
Parsley sprig
1 teaspoon salt
1 teaspoon pepper
2 quarts water

Step II:
1 head cabbage, cut in 8 wedges
2 onions, sliced
2 cups diced potatoes
8 small carrots, sliced
2 stalks celery, sliced
Cut-up cooked chicken (from Step I)
1 cup peas

Put the chicken and the giblets in a large pot. Add all other ingredients in Step I and bring to a boil. Simmer for 30 minutes. Refrigerate the chicken and when cool remove the meat from the bones. Discard the bones and strain the broth. Heat the strained broth in a large saucepan. Add the cabbage, onions, potatoes, carrots, and celery. Simmer for 20 minutes, or until the vegetables are crisp. Add the chicken pieces and peas and cook for 5 minutes longer. Serve in large soup bowls. Serves 4–6.

BAVARIAN CABBAGE SOUP

3 pounds soup bones, such as shank, plate, or leg bones
2 cups shredded cabbage
1 cup diced turnips
1 cup diced carrots
1 cup cut string beans
1 cup green peas
1 cup onions, sliced
1 tablespoon salt
2 teaspoons pepper
4 tablespoons flour
4 tablespoons butter

Cover soup bones with water and boil slowly for about 2 hours. Add cabbage, turnips, carrots, string beans, peas, and onions. Season with salt and pepper; simmer for another 45 minutes. In a heavy frying pan brown the flour by stirring frequently to prevent burning until it turns a dark brown color. Add the butter to the browned flour and blend well. Thin the paste with a little meat stock and pour the sauce back into the pot of soup. Heat and serve with rye bread and butter.

This browned flour and butter gravy sauce is called Einbrenne in German cooking. It has a distinct brown color and a slightly bitter flavor. You should brown the flour according to your own taste.

IRISH CABBAGE SOUP

3 pounds beef or veal bones
1 medium head cabbage, chopped
2 cups canned tomatoes
2 cups chopped celery
1 cup chopped onion
1 tablespoon salt
1 teaspoon pepper
2 quarts water
2 cups mashed potatoes

Cook the meat bones, salt, and pepper in the water in a large pot for 2 to 3 hours. Add the cabbage, tomatoes, celery, and onion and cook 20 minutes longer. Serve very hot over mashed potatoes. Serves 6.

SPANISH BOILED DINNER

    1 pound dried chick peas
    1 pound pork jowl, cut in 1-inch pieces
    1 pound soup meat, such as beef
    2 pounds beef bones, cut or cracked
    2 tablespoons salt
    1 head cabbage, cut in wedges
    3 large carrots, cut up
    6 potatoes, peeled and quartered
    4 ribs celery, cut in half
4–5 sprigs parsley
    2 pounds hot Spanish sausage
    2 cloves garlic
    1 pound thin spaghetti

Place the chick peas in a large pot, cover with water and let stand 1 day. Drain off the original water, cover the peas with 2 quarts of fresh water, add 1 tablespoon of salt, and simmer for 1 hour.

Put all of the meat and bones in a large kettle and cover with water. Add 1 tablespoon of salt and simmer slowly for 1 hour. Add all other ingredients to the pot and boil for another hour. (Do not add the spaghetti until the last few minutes.) Remove as many of the bones as possible. Combine the drained chick peas with the other vegetables and meat and serve in large plates as a very thick soup. Serves 8.

CABBAGE AND POTATO SOUP

2 tablespoons butter or margarine
1 medium onion, diced fine
2 cups cabbage, shredded fine
2 cups potato, diced fine
2 cups water
2 cups cream
1 teaspoon salt
1 teaspoon pepper
1 teaspoon paprika
Dash cayenne
1 cup croutons for topping

Prepare croutons and set aside for last-minute serving. Melt margarine in saucepan and sauté the onions until golden brown. Add remaining ingredients. Simmer for 30 to 40 minutes. Serve hot with croutons. Serves 4–5.

GALICIAN SOUP
(Spanish)

1 cup dried white beans
12 cups water
1 pound beef, cubed
1 pound smoked ham, cubed
¼ pound salt pork, diced
1 chicken, cut in small pieces
2 tablespoons salt
1 tablespoon pepper
2 cups canned tomatoes
4 cups diced and peeled potatoes
2 cups diced and peeled turnips
1 large onion, chopped
1 small head cabbage, cored and cut into 1-inch squares
1 clove garlic, diced
Pinch ground cloves
Parsley sprig

Pick over the beans and soak them in a large kettle in 6 cups of water for 1 hour. Drain off the water and add 6 cups of fresh water. Bring to a boil and simmer the beans for 1 hour. Add the beef, ham, and pork and simmer for 1 hour. Add all other ingredients and simmer 45 minutes longer, until all ingredients are tender and the soup is well blended. Serve with crusty Italian bread. Serves 8.

POLISH BORSCHT

3–4 pounds beef shin bones
  1 tablespoon salt
  2 cups tomato purée
  1 carrot, grated
  1 large onion, diced fine
  1 medium cabbage, finely shredded
  1 cup diced green pepper
  2 cups beets with their liquid, grated or diced fine
Fresh dill, chopped
Sour cream

Place the beef in a large kettle and cover with water. Salt to taste and boil for 2 to 3 hours. Remove as much of the meat from the bones as possible. Skim the surface if necessary and add the tomato purée, carrot, onion, cabbage, green pepper, beets, and dill. Simmer another 30 to 45 minutes. Remove the dill and serve the soup in bowls with the sour cream spooned on top. Meat shreds can be used in the soup. Serves 8.

GREEK CABBAGE SOUP

 3 pounds lamb bones
 1 medium head cabbage, shredded
 3 tart apples, chopped
 2 onions, chopped
 2 cups tomatoes
¼ cup lemon juice
 1 tablespoon salt
 1 teaspoon pepper
 1 tablespoon sugar
 3 tablespoons flour

Place the lamb bones in a large pot, add 3 quarts water. Simmer for 2 hours or more. Add all ingredients except flour. Cook for another hour. By this time the meat should fall off the bones. Remove the bones from the pot. Make a paste with the flour and a little cold water. Add to the pot of soup and stir until slightly thickened and smooth. Serves 6–8.

CREAM OF CABBAGE SOUP

1 cup cabbage
1 cup sauerkraut
1 quart stock from cooking cabbage
3 eggs
1 cup cream
3 tablespoons butter
3 tablespoons flour

Cook the cabbage and sauerkraut in 2 quarts of water for 1 hour. Leave in cooking stock. Beat eggs and mix in the cream. Mix flour with ½ cup cold water to make a paste, stir into egg mixture. Drop butter into cabbage mixture, stir in the egg and flour paste. Stir over low heat until thickened. Season with your favorite spice: salt, pepper, anise, mustard, or caraway seeds to taste. Serves 4–6.

THICK CABBAGE SOUP

Meat bone or ham hock
½ cup barley
½ head medium cabbage, shredded
6–8 medium potatoes, finely diced
Salt
Pepper

Cook the barley with bone or ham hock in 2 quarts of water for 1 hour. Add the shredded cabbage and the potatoes. Season with salt and pepper. Cook until very soft (for about another hour). When tender, serve hot with rye bread and butter. Serves 8–10.

70

HUNGARIAN HEROES
(Submarines)

I: Hard roll
Roast turkey, sliced thin
Roast beef, sliced thin
Swiss cheese, sliced thin
Cole slaw with dressing

II: Pastrami slices
Rye bread
Cole slaw with dressing
Sliced Swiss cheese

III: Rye bread
Corned beef
Cole slaw with dressing with mustard sauce
Cheese

IV: Roast beef
American cheese
White bread
Cole slaw

V: Hot sauerkraut
Rye bread
Hot sliced frankfurters
Sauce of oil, dry mustard mixture

VI: Liverwurst
Sauerkraut
Mustard sauce
Rye bread

Open-face sandwich:
Place layer of sauerkraut on rye bread. Slice liverwurst and spread mustard. Place under broiler 3 minutes to heat.

71

VII: Rye bread
Knockwurst (hot)
Sauerkraut (hot)

Boil knockwurst and slice. Heat sauerkraut and spread over rye bread.

VIII: Sliced turkey (roll is okay), heated if desired
Hot slaw with mustard dressing
Sliced ham, heated if desired
Hard roll or rye bread
Thin slice of melon

XI: Sliced turkey, heated
Boiled cabbage, heated
Cheese or heavy cheese sauce
Bread

Place hot turkey on slice of bread, spread some boiled cabbage and a slice of cheese or sauce over top. Broil 3 minutes to brown.

X: Hard roll
Pepperoni slices
Cole slaw
Cheese slices

SUMMER SLAW
FOR OUTDOOR PICNIC SANDWICHES

    3 cups shredded cabbage (very fine shred)
    ¼ teaspoon caraway seeds
    2 tablespoons finely minced onions
    2 tablespoons vinegar
    3 tablespoons cream
    ½ cup mayonnaise or salad dressing
    3 teaspoons dry mustard

Mix mustard with mayonnaise, cream, and vinegar. Toss the finely minced onion with the finely shredded cabbage and the caraway seeds. Add only enough dressing to moisten; toss well. Save the rest of the dressing to be used in making picnic sandwiches as suggested below.

Suggested ingredients for picnic sandwiches:
Rye bread, buttered slices
Swiss cheese, sliced thin
Corned beef, sliced thin
Roast beef, sliced thin
Turkey, sliced thin
Bermuda onion, sliced thin
Pepperoni, sliced very thin
Recipe of summer slaw
Dressing

Let each person select the meats, cheese, or other foods which he wishes in order to make a delicious sandwich for an easy picnic.

Cabbage Rolls from Many Nations

Travelers around the world find variations of the cabbage roll. The ingredients—the meat, the cereal, the spices, and sauces—vary to enhance the flavors and to impart distinction of origin. For cabbage rolls are from all nations. "The finest meal in one," proclaim the cooks who practice the art of cabbage-roll cooking.

The art is easy. A few basic steps are as follows.

Select firm and clean cabbage.

Soften leaves by boiling the entire head of cabbage in a very large pot for 15 minutes; then pull off each leaf as needed. Another method of softening is to core the cabbage head, remove leaf by leaf, and immerse each leaf in hot water for about 3 minutes. Either method is easy. Remove the rib around the cabbage center before rolling.

Use about 2 tablespoons of mixture for each leaf. Roll the leaf to form a square-looking ball, secure the leaf with toothpicks, or simply place open side down and the leaf will remain closed.

After all filling has been used, pour on the appropriate sauce, cover and bake at 350° for one hour or simmer covered on top of the stove for 45 minutes.

Delicious as leftovers, cabbage rolls freeze beautifully and keep for several weeks in the freezer.

SHRIMP FILLING IN CABBAGE ROLLS

Filling:
    1 onion, minced
    1 tablespoon margarine
    1 pound shrimp
    2 cups cooked rice
    ½ cup bouillon
    ½ tablespoon parsley
    1 teaspoon salt
    ½ teaspoon pepper
    1 egg
    ½ tablespoon curry powder

Sauce:
    1 tablespoon curry powder
    ½ cup water

Sauté the onion in the margarine. Mix with the other ingredients and make the cabbage rolls. Place the rolls in a saucepan with a cover. Pour the sauce over the rolls and cook, covered, over low heat for 45 minutes. Serves 4–5.

CHILI BEANS IN CABBAGE ROLLS

Filling:
    1 onion, minced
    ½ stick margerine
    1 pound ground chuck
    1 pound bulk pork sausage meat
    1 cup raw rice
    1 can (about 2 cups) Mexican Chili Beans
    ½ tablespoon chili powder
    ¼ teaspoon cumin

Sauce:
1 can tomato soup
1 soup can water
1 teaspoon salt
1 teaspoon pepper
1 tablespoon chili powder
1 teaspoon cumin
2 tablespoons steak sauce
2 tablespoons honey (optional)

Sauté the onion in the margarine. Add the meats, rice, beans, and spices. Make the cabbage rolls. Make the sauce and pour over the cabbage rolls. Cook, covered, for 1 hour. Serves 8.

STUFFED CABBAGE WITH ITALIAN SAUSAGE AND ROSEMARY

  8 cabbage leaves, wilted
  1 pound bulk hot sausage
  1 clove garlic, minced
  ½ teaspoon dried rosemary
  ½ cup chopped parsley
  1 cup bread crumbs
  1 egg
  ½ cup heavy cream
  ½ cup Parmeasan cheese
  2 tablespoons white wine
  ½ cup tomato purée

Sauté the sausage until done; pour off excess fat. Add the garlic, rosemary, parsley, cream, bread crumbs, egg, salt and pepper to taste. Blend the mixture well, form into balls, roll in the cabbage leaves. Place the cabbage rolls in a greased casserole, sprinkle with the cheese and bake at 350° for 25–30 minutes. Mix the wine and tomato purée, simmer a few minutes and serve as a sauce over the cabbage rolls. Serves 4.

SWEDISH CABBAGE ROLLS

Filling:
  2 cups raw rice
  1 cup milk
  1 cup water
  1 pound ground beef
  ½ pound ground pork
  ½ pound ground veal
  2 teaspoons salt
  1 teaspoon pepper
  1 egg, beaten
  1 teaspoon thyme
  ½ stick margarine
  3 tablespoons flour
  1 cup beef bouillon

Sauce:
  1 cup sour cream
  2 tablespoons horseradish
  ½ cup fresh chopped scallions
  ¼ teaspoon cardamon

Cook the rice in the milk and water for 5 to 8 minutes only. Mix in the meats, salt, pepper, beaten egg, and thyme. If too moist to handle, add some bread crumbs. Make up the cabbage rolls. Heat the margarine in a heavy skillet and brown the rolls on all sides. Transfer the rolls to a covered casserole as they are browned. After all the rolls have been browned, sprinkle the flour into the skillet with the fat and the pan juices from the meat. Stir until blended and slightly brown. Add the bouillon and stir until smooth. Pour over the cabbage rolls in the casserole. Cover and bake 1 hour at 350°. Mix the sauce and serve spooned over the hot cabbage rolls. Serves 6–8.

AMERICAN-STYLE CABBAGE ROLLS

Filling:
- 1 pound ground beef
- 1 onion, minced
- 2 cups minute rice
- 1 egg
- ½ teaspoon pepper
- 1 teaspoon salt
- 1 tablespoon Worcestershire sauce
- ¼ teaspoon garlic powder

Sauce:
- 1 can tomatoes
- 1 bay leaf
- Garlic on a pick
- 1 teaspoon salt
- ½ teaspoon pepper

Mix filling ingredients together and make cabbage rolls. Pour mixed sauce over and simmer, covered, for 45 minutes. Serves 4–5.

SYRIAN STUFFED CABBAGE

Filling:
- 1 garlic clove, put through press
- 2 tablespoons olive oil
- 2 pounds lamb, ground
- 1 cup raw rice
- 2 teaspoons salt
- ½ teaspoon allspice
- ½ cup tomato sauce
- ½ cup lemon juice
- 1 tablespoon dried mint

Sauce:
- 1 cup tomato sauce
- 1 clove garlic
- ¼ cup lemon juice
- ¼ cup olive oil

Garnish:
White grapes
Dried mint

Sauté the garlic in the olive oil for two minutes. Add the lamb and sauté for a few minutes. Mix the remaining ingredients and make up the cabbage rolls. Combine the ingredients for the sauce and pour over the cabbage rolls. Cover and bake for 1 hour at 350°. Just before serving, garnish with a sprinkle of the mint and the white grapes. Serves 8.

GREAT WESTERN MEAT AND CABBAGE ROLLS
(Open Fire Method)

Filling:
- 1 pound ground beef
- 1 pound ground pork
- 3 cups cooked rice
- 1 tablespoon salt
- 1 teaspoon pepper
- 1 cup minced onions
- 1 egg
- ½ teaspoon cumin
- 1 tablespoon chili powder

Sauce:
- 2 cups tomato sauce
- 2 tablespoons molasses
- 2 tablespoons lemon juice
- 1 teaspoon chili powder
- Dash of cumin

Mix filling ingredients together and make up cabbage rolls. Put rolls seam side down in a skillet. Mix sauce ingredients together and pour over the rolls. Cook, covered, on top of the stove for 1 hour. Baste often. Serves 8.

DUTCH CABBAGE ROLLS

Filling:
1 cup raw rice
2 tablespoons cooking oil
1 onion, minced
2 pounds ground beef
2 teaspoons salt
1 teaspoon pepper
1 egg
1 teaspoon poppy seeds

Sauce:
  1 can tomato soup
  1 soup can water
  1 teaspoon parsley flakes
  1 teaspoon celery seeds
  2 tablespoons lemon juice
  1 teaspoon salt
½ teaspoon pepper
½ teaspoon garlic powder

Garnish:
Bacon bits

Cook the rice in salted water for 8–10 minutes. Rinse and drain. Sauté the onion in the oil for a few minutes. Mix the rice, sautéed onion, and all the other filling ingredients together and make up the cabbage rolls. Mix the sauce and pour over the cabbage rolls. Cover and bake at 350° for 1 hour. Garnish with the bacon bits. Spoon sauce over each serving. Serves 8.

CABBAGE ROLLS WITH CHICKEN FILLING
(Hungarian)

    3 cups cooked chicken, diced (canned can be used)
    1 cup bread crumbs
    2 tablespoons fresh onion, minced
    ½ cup celery, minced
    ½ cup mushrooms, chopped
    ¼ teaspoon garlic powder
    ½ teaspoon salt
    ¼ teaspoon poultry seasoning
    1 egg
    1 teaspoon pepper
    2 cups chicken broth

Sauce:
    1 cup sour cream
    1 cup chicken broth
    3 tablespoons flour
    1 tablespoon paprika
    ½ stick margarine
    1 cup water
Pepper

Mix together all ingredients for the filling. If too moist add more bread crumbs. Make up the cabbage rolls and pour some chicken broth over the top. Bake, covered; at 350° for about 45 minutes.

Make the sauce. Melt margarine, add the flour, and both the broth and the cream. Flavor with salt, paprika, and pepper and stir until thickened. Spoon sauce over each cabbage roll at serving time. Serves 5–6.

BAKED PIROGI
(Piroshki)

2 sticks margarine
3 cups flour
½ cup cream
1 teaspoon salt
1 egg

Cream the margarine and flour together. Add salt and cream. Blend well until the consistency of good pie pastry. Roll out dough between waxed paper, taking a large handful of dough (1 cup) at a time. Cut into 3-inch squares or use a glass about 3 inches in diameter and cut out shapes. Combine the egg with a tablespoon of water. Place 1 tablespoon (or less) of filling on each piece of pastry. Fold over and brush lightly with the egg mixture to help seal the edges. These will be crescent shaped or triangle shaped. Place on a baking sheet. When finished, brush with the egg mixture. Slash a small hole in each piroshki or prick with a fork. Bake at 350° until golden brown, usually 15 minutes. Three cups of flour will make 35–40 pieces of pastry.

Filling #1:
- 2 grated onions
- ½ stick butter
- 1 pound finely ground beef or pork sausage
- ¼ cup sour cream
- 2 cups cooked rice
- 1 teaspoon salt
- ½ teaspoon pepper
- 1 teaspoon Worcestershire sauce
- 2 cups cooked, shredded cabbage

May be further seasoned with parsley flakes, dill, or other spices as desired. Sauté onions in butter. Add beef and sauté until browned. Mix in all other ingredients and fill the pastry for baking.

Filling #2:
- 1 onion, minced
- ¼ stick margarine
- 3 cups minced, chopped ham
- 3 cups chopped, cooked cabbage
- 3 cups cooked rice
- 2 teaspoons salt
- 1 teaspoon pepper
- 1 tablespoon mustard
- 1 egg

Sauté onion in margarine; add other ingredients and fill Piroshki.

Filling #3:
- 3 cups cooked cabbage
- 1 cup cottage cheese
- 1 onion, minced and sautéed
- Salt
- Pepper

Serve with sour cream as sauce.

Filling #4:
4 cups cooked cabbage
1 cup shrimp, cut up, cooked
Salt
Pepper
Serve hot with hot prepared mustard sauce or a hot curry sauce.

Filling #5:
3 cups sauerkraut, drained and dry
1 cup applesauce
Serve with cinnamon powder.

Filling #6:
3 cups fried cabbage
2 cups instant potatoes or mashed potato
Salt
Pepper
Serve with butter sauce.

Filling #7:
3 cups cooked cabbage
1 pound pork sausage
Salt
Pepper
Serve with fried apples.

Filling #8:
2 cups sauerkraut
1 cup mashed potatoes
1 cup cottage cheese
Serve with sour cream.

Filling #9:
3 cups cooked cabbage
½ cup raisins
Serve with butter sauce.

Relishes

KIM CHEE

1 head Chinese cabbage
2 tablespoons salt
1 quart water
1½ tablespoons hot pepper, ground
1 clove garlic, minced
1 teaspoon ginger
1 tablespoon sugar
2 scallions, cut

Cut Chinese cabbage into 1 inch pieces. Sprinkle with salt and cover with water. Let stand several hours.

Mix remaining spices together and let them stand blending. Drain cabbage and rinse well. Sprinkle the spices over the leaves, pack into a jar and allow to stand for 3 to 4 days before using. Will keep for several days.

NEW ENGLAND CABBAGE RELISH

    1 head cabbage, shredded
    2 green peppers, shredded
    2 sour pickles, cut fine
    ½ cup olives, cut fine
    ½ cup pimientos
    ½ teaspoon celery seed
    ¼ teaspoon garlic salt
    ½ cup olive oil
    ½ cup vinegar
    1 teaspoon salt
    1 teaspoon pepper
    1 teaspoon sugar

Combine all vegetables. Mix the dressing and pour over the vegetable mixture. Allow to stand for 2 to 3 days. Delicious with meats.

SOUTHERN SWEET CABBAGE RELISH

4 cups chopped cabbage
2 cups chopped sweet red peppers
2 cups chopped green peppers
2 cups chopped onions
1 quart cider vinegar
3 tablespoons salt
1 cup sugar
2 tablespoons mustard seed
2 tablespoons celery seed
1 tablespoon tumeric

Remove seeds from the peppers and chop with the other vegetables. Add the spices and vinegar. Let mixture stand overnight in an enamel or covered glass jar. Pack into sterilized jars and process in water bath, simmering for 30 minutes. Be sure seals are tight after cooling. Store in cool place.

RED CABBAGE RELISH

1 head red cabbage, finely shredded
½ cup salt
5 cups vinegar
¼ cup whole cloves
1 teaspoon pepper corns
1 teaspoon allspice
1 tablespoon celery seed

Put the shredded cabbage in an earthen jar. Sprinkle with salt. Let stand 1 day. Rinse with clear water. Tie the spices in a cloth (nylon net) and boil in vinegar for 10 minutes. Cool vinegar and pour over the cabbage in the jar. Cover jar loosely and let it stand for 3 to 4 days before using. Will keep several weeks. Makes 2–3 quarts.

MARINATED CABBAGE-CAULIFLOWER

4 cups chopped cabbage
2 cups cauliflower buds
2 teaspoons salt
2 cups juice from any processed pickles or cucumbers

Chop cabbage in large pieces. Remove cauliflower buds and cut in bite-sized pieces. Sprinkle with salt and let stand for 1 hour. Rinse off salt and pour on the juice from any jar of leftover dill pickles, sweet pickles, olives, or Kosher pickles. Place in covered jar in refrigerator. Let marinate for at least 2 days. Will keep for over 1 week while covered and refrigerated.

Brussels Sprouts

BRUSSELS SPROUTS AUSTRIAN STYLE

1 package frozen Brussels sprouts
4–5 slices bacon
1 teaspoon salt
¼ cup honey
2 tablespoons vinegar
Pimiento slices
2 tablespoons cornstarch

Fry bacon in skillet until crisp while Brussels sprouts are boiling in separate sauce pan. Drain bacon on absorbent paper. Add spices, along with vinegar and pimiento to drippings in pan. Mix cornstarch with ¼ cup cold water and add to pan, stirring until thickened. Add sprouts and heat through. Sprinkle crumbled bacon into sauce just before serving. Serve immediately. Serves 4.

BRUSSELS SPROUTS IN BUTTER SAUCE

1 package frozen Brussels sprouts
½ teaspoon salt
2 tablespoons butter
1 teaspoon lemon juice

Boil the Brussels sprouts in salted water for about 15 minutes. Toss with butter and lemon juice. Serves 4.

99

BRUSSELS SPROUTS WITH
CREAM CHEESE SAUCE

1 package frozen Brussels sprouts
4 ounces cream cheese
1 cup milk
1 apple, diced
¼ teaspoon nutmeg
½ teaspoon salt
Dash pepper

Boil sprouts for about 10 minutes. Melt cheese in top of double boiler over simmering water. Add apples, milk, and spices. When cheese has melted smooth, pour over cooked sprouts. Serves 4.

POTATO SALAD WITH BRUSSELS SPROUTS

1 tablespoon minced parsley
2 tablespoons lemon juice
1 teaspoon salt
½ teaspoon pepper
½ cup oil
½ cup mayonnaise
2 tablespoons grated cheese, Parmesan or Romano
4 cups of cooked potato, diced in large chunks
1 cup Brussels sprouts, cooked tender / crisp

Mix a dressing of the mayonnaise, oil, salt, pepper, cheese, lemon juice, and parsley. Add potatoes and sprouts to the dressing and toss. Cover and refrigerate. Serves 6–8.

Sauerkraut Dishes

SAUERKRAUT

This versatile vegetable can be purchased commercially or it can be made at home and kept in jars or frozen.

The method of preparing sauerkraut depends on your own preference. Some families use it from the can—tart, sour, and strong. Others like to drain and wash the brine from the kraut. Flavor and food value are in the liquid, so my advice is to be wary and not pour too much nutrition down the drain.

Sauerkraut mixes well with many fruits, either sweet or sour. Vegetables blend in with the sauerkraut and any spice that may please your fancy. To modify the flavor of kraut, homemakers can use oatmeal or instant potatoes. To enhance or sharpen the kraut flavor, use more lemon or vinegar.

In making up a dish with sauerkraut, double the recipe and save leftovers for another day since the flavors are enriched by standing.

102

HOMEMADE SAUERKRAUT

10 pounds of cabbage
½ cup salt

Get a large crock to hold 8 quarts. Wash and scald thoroughly. Remove the outer leaves from the cabbage but do not wash the heads. The heads have natural wild yeast and if this is washed off the sauerkraut will not ferment properly. Shred the cabbage directly into the crock. For each 2 inches of cabbage, sprinkle a tablespoon of salt. Pack down well with a potato masher or glass jar. Continue making the layers. When finished, cover the container with a clean white cloth. Find a plate that nearly fits the top of the crock and place this inverted, on the shredded cabbage. Weight the plate down with a piece of limestone. The weight of the stone will hold the cabbage under the brine that will form in 3 to 4 days. A small amount of lime is dissolved by the brine and this aids in the lactic acid fermentation that gives sauerkraut its flavor. Allow it to ferment for 4 to 6 weeks in a cool place below 60° F. Skim off the film that may form during fermentation. The kraut can be kept in the crock for 4 months or more. Kraut can be frozen, if desired, or canned by packing tightly into sterilized jars and sealed. Fermentation will stop while frozen. Ten pounds of cabbage makes about 8 quarts of sauerkraut.

SAUERKRAUT VIENNESE

　4　cups sauerkraut
　¼　teaspoon ground cloves
　1　bay leaf
　½　teaspoon salt
　1　cup sour cream
　1　pound sausage links or patties

　Place sauerkraut, cloves, bay leaf, and salt in a saucepan. Cook until liquid has almost evaporated. Remove the bay leaf and add the sour cream slowly. Put in a baking dish and place the sausage links or patties over the top of the kraut. Bake at 350° for 30 minutes. Serves 4–6.

SAUTEED SWEET SAUERKRAUT

　1　onion, minced
　3　tablespoons bacon fat or butter
　1　quart sauerkraut
　1　raw potato, grated
　1　teaspoon caraway seeds
　1　tablespoon honey or brown sugar

　Melt the fat or butter. Sauté the onion until slightly golden. Add the sauerkraut, caraway seeds, and potato in a covered kettle over low heat. Brown sugar or honey can be added the last few minutes of cooking. Serves 6.

SAUERKRAUT WITH NOODLES

  2 cups of noodles
  4 cups water
  ½ tablespoon salt
  1 onion minced
  4 tablespoons butter or lard
  4 cups drained sauerkraut
  4 cups diced ham
  ½ teaspoon pepper
Spices, such as caraway, aniseed, or parsley flakes

Cook the noodles in the water with the salt. Drain. Sauté the onion in the butter or lard. Add the drained noodles and toss until the noodles are golden. Add the sauerkraut and sauté for 5 minutes. Add all other ingredients and put in a greased baking dish. Bake for 15 minutes at 350° or until the sauerkraut has dried out a little. Serve with fried liver sausage or German bloodwurst. Serves 6–8.

POTATO KRAUT FROM THE RHINELAND
1 can sauerkraut
2 cups sliced cooked potatoes
1 onion, chopped
1 cup sour cream
1 ounce pimento strips
1 tablespoon dry mustard
1 teaspoon salt
½ teaspoon pepper
¼ teaspoon celery seed
¼ teaspoon caraway seed
1 cup milk
Scallions
Radishes, sliced

Rinse sauerkraut. Mix all items together and toss well.
Heat in saucepan over low heat and serve. Serves 4–6.

SAUERKRAUT WITH PEA PUREE

1 pound split peas, green or yellow
4 cups sauerkraut
1 medium onion
Salt and pepper

Simmer split peas until completely disintegrated so that
they form a purée. Add the sauerkraut and minced onion.
Simmer another 30 to 40 minutes. Season with pepper
and salt if desired. This recipe is enhanced by reheating.
It keeps well for several days.

106

SAUERKRAUT WITH CHEESE SAUCE

½ stick margarine
2 tablespoons flour
½ teaspoon salt
¼ teaspoon pepper
1 teaspoon dry mustard
1 teaspoon steak sauce
1 cup milk
1 cup shredded Cheddar or American cheese
1 can (2 pounds) sauerkraut
1 cup fine dry bread crumbs mixed with ¼ cup shred-
    ded cheese

Melt margarine in saucepan and stir in flour, salt, pepper, mustard, and steak sauce. Add milk slowly and stir
until slightly thickened. Add cheese, stir until melted and
thick. Drain sauerkraut, rinse if desired. Put into greased
casserole dish and pour sauce over. Sprinkle the bread
crumb and cheese mixture over the top. Bake at 350° for
30 minutes, until top is brown and bubbles have formed.
Serves 4–6.

APRICOT-FLAVORED SAUERKRAUT

1 can sauerkraut
1 cup beef stock or soup
2 tablespoons margarine
½ teaspoon poppy seeds, if desired, or ¼ tsp. aniseed
½ teaspoon salt
3 tablespoons honey or sorghum
1 cup dry apricots, soaked in water 2 to 3 hours

Combine all ingredients in a large skillet and heat slowly, mixing frequently. Cook about 30 minutes. Serve hot. Serves 6.

SAUERKRAUT WITH TOMATOES

6–8 slices bacon
½ cup chopped onion
½ teaspoon salt
2 tablespoons honey
1 cup tomato sauce
1 can (1 pound) sauerkraut
Dry, herb-seasoned bread stuffing
Margarine

Dice the bacon and fry until crisp. Remove from pan and drain on absorbent paper. Drain most of the bacon fat from the pan, add the onion and sauté until tender. Add the salt, honey, and tomato sauce and heat over a low flame for about 10 minutes. Add the sauerkraut and bacon bits and pour into a casserole. Sprinkle herb-seasoned bread stuffing mix over the top and dot with margarine. Bake at 350° for 30–35 minutes. Serves 4–6.

SPICY SWISS KRAUT

  2 tablespoons oil
  ½ cup chopped onion
  1 clove garlic, minced
  ½ cup chopped green pepper
  1 quart sauerkraut, drained
  1 cup broth
  ½ teaspoon paprika
  ½ teaspoon salt
Dash pepper
  ½ teaspoon dried dill
  1 cup drained canned tomatoes
  2 tablespoons flour
6–7 boiled, peeled potatoes
  1 pound bulk sausage or frankfurters

Sauté onion, garlic, and pepper in a little oil. Add the kraut, broth, and all other ingredients except the flour. Simmer for about 30 minutes. Mix the flour with a little water and add to pot. Transfer to a casserole, top with boiled potatoes and sausage patties or frankfurters. Bake for 15 minutes at 400°. To get a more bitter flavor, flour can be pan-browned before adding to kraut. Serves 6.

Sauerkraut with Meat

PORK CHOP AND APPLE KRAUT DINNER

8 pork chops, ¾-inch thick
Shortening
1 teaspoon salt
½ teaspoon pepper
3–4 cups sauerkraut
1 teaspoon caraway seed
½ cup brown sugar
¼ cup chopped onion
1 cup chopped apples

Brown the pork chops well in the shortening in a skillet or Dutch oven. Season with the salt and pepper. Mix sauerkraut with all other ingredients and place in a pan with a cover. Lay pork chops on top, cover, and cook over low heat for at least 1 hour. Baste with the juices to keep chops moist. Allow 1–2 chops per serving.

PORK WITH SAUERKRAUT
(Russian)

1 cup raw rice
2 teaspoons salt
½ teaspoon caraway seeds
1 tablespoon honey
1 apple, diced
½ cup flour
1 teaspoon pepper
1 tablespoon sweet paprika
½ cup shortening
2 pounds lean pork, cut in 1-inch cubes
2 large onions, chopped
1 cup water, plus more if needed
1 pound Polish sausage, cut in 1-inch pieces
1 cup sour cream

Cook the rice in slightly salted (1 teaspoon salt) water for about 10 minutes. Rinse and drain. Drain the sauerkraut and mix in the caraway seeds, honey, and diced apple. Mix the flour with 1 teaspoon salt and the pepper and paprika. Heat the shortening in a skillet. Dredge the pork cubes in the flour mixture and brown the meat on all sides. Add the onions and cook for about 5 minutes. Add 1 cup of water to the saucepan and simmer for about 30 minutes. Remove the meat and onions. Add the remaining flour to the liquid in the pan and brown slightly. Add enough water to make a light gravy. Heat the oven to 350°.

Grease a large casserole and make layers of the ingredients. First place a layer of sauerkraut followed by layers of pork cubes, rice, and sausage. Repeat the layers a second time. Pour the gravy over the entire dish. Bake for 35 minutes or until the top is crisp and browned. Serve each portion topped with a dab of sour cream. Serves 6–8.

SMOKED PORK LOIN WITH SAUERKRAUT

3-pound pork loin, smoked (about a 6-inch piece)
1 bay leaf
4 whole allspice
½ teaspoon peppercorns
4 cups sauerkraut
1 large onion, minced
3 slices bacon
1 cup diced apples
¼ cup brown sugar
½ cup dry white wine

Place pork loin in large kettle and cover with water. Add the bay leaf, allspice, and peppercorns. Boil over low heat for 1 hour. (It must be a genuine smoked loin and not one that has been treated by other means.) Preheat oven to 350°. Use baking pan and sauté the minced onions, bacon, and apples for about 10 minutes. Remove from heat and add the brown sugar, sauerkraut, and wine. Remove pork loin from the cooking water and place it on top of the sauerkraut. Add one cup of the liquid from the pot. Bake at 350° for 45 minutes, basting every few minutes. Use more of the cooking water if necessary to baste the pork loin. Serve with boiled potatoes and homemade sweet bread. Serves 4–5.

PORK CHOPS WITH SAUERKRAUT
AND TOMATO SAUCE

4 thick pork chops (1 per portion)
1 quart sauerkraut
1 can tomatoes (2 cups)
1 teaspoon salt
1 tablespoon paprika
⅛ teaspoon aniseed (optional)

Brown the chops in a frying pan and place them in the bottom of a buttered casserole dish. Cover with the sauerkraut and the tomatoes. Sprinkle with salt, paprika, and aniseed if desired. Cover and simmer for about 1 hour or bake at 350° for 1½ hours. Serves 4.

PORK AND SAUERKRAUT
HUNGARIAN GOULASH

2½–3 pounds boneless pork, such as shoulder
2 cups onions
1 clove garlic, chopped
1 tablespoon salt
1 tablespoon meat sauce
1 cup water
3½ cups sauerkraut
Dill or caraway seed
2 cups sour cream
1 tablespoon paprika

Wipe meat and cut in 1½-inch cubes. Remove as much fat as possible. In a large covered saucepan or Dutch oven, combine all ingredients except the cream and the paprika. Cook over medium heat for 1 hour or until meat is tender. Remove from heat and stir in the sour cream and paprika. Heat through but do not boil. Serves 6.

BAKED SPARERIBS AND SAUERKRAUT WITH DUMPLINGS

3–4 pounds spareribs
Salt
Pepper
Paprika
  1 quart sauerkraut

Dumplings:
  2 cups sifted flour (may use one cup corn meal and
     one cup flour)
2½ tablespoons baking powder
  1 egg
 ½ teaspoon salt
 ¾ cup milk

Cut spareribs into individual portions. Season with salt, pepper, and paprika. Cover with the sauerkraut and bake covered for 2 hours at 350°. Remove cover and bake another 20 minutes. Mix all ingredients for the dumplings and beat until there are no lumps. Drop by spoonfuls on top of sauerkraut and bake uncovered for another 15 minutes at 400°.

TENDERLOIN OF PORK WITH KRAUT DRESSING

2 pork tenderloins (4-inch cuts)
1 can sauerkraut
2 cups toasted bread crumbs
1 tablespoon chopped celery
1 medium onion, chopped
1 stick margarine
1 teaspoon salt
½ teaspoon poultry seasoning
¼ teaspoon pepper
1 egg
Other spices as desired

Mix the sauerkraut with all ingredients, except the pork. Place this stuffing in the hollow parts of the tenderloins. Tie together, insert meat thermometer into tenderloin and bake until meat is done. Roast at 325° about 25 minutes to the pound. Serves 8.

SAUERKRAUT WITH PIG HOCKS

3–4 pounds pig hocks or feet
Salt
Pepper
1 quart sauerkraut, drained

Select pig hocks that look meaty. Put in a large pot with plenty of water, salt, and pepper. Cook about 3 hours or more. Add sauerkraut and cook for another 45 minutes. Serve the dish with pumpernickel bread on the side. Or, as an added touch, you can top the dish with mashed potatoes. Serves 6–8.

GERMAN KRAUT DINNER IN SKILLET

1 pound frankfurters
1 apple, diced
1 potato, diced
2 cups undrained sauerkraut
1 teaspoon caraway seed
½ cup water

In large saucepan, heat frankfurters and brown very lightly. Mix the apple with the potato and spread over the frankfurters. Top with sauerkraut and sprinkle with caraway seed. Add enough water to keep from burning. Cover and simmer for 15 to 20 minutes. Serves 6.

FRANKFURTERS IN CROWN AROUND SAUERKRAUT

12–20 good frankfurters
1½ quarts sauerkraut, drained
Pepper
Butter or bacon drippings
Caraway seeds
2 cups mashed potatoes

Cut frankfurters in half. In a large, flat-bottomed casserole dish place the frankfurters standing up along the edge, the cut side down. Toothpicks can be used to make the frankfurters stand up against each other. Follow the pattern around the casserole to form the crown. Season the sauerkraut with pepper and butter, if desired, and caraway and mix with the mashed potatoes. Place the mixture in the center of the crown of frankfurters. Bake at 350° for 30 minutes. Serve with hot rye bread and butter. Serves 8–12.

KNOCKWURST WITH KRAUT

1 can frozen apple juice (6 ounces)
1 juice can water
6 dried apricots
6 dried pitted prunes
2 dried pears or apples, diced
1 onion, sliced
½ stick margarine
6 knockwurst sliced
3 cups (#2½ can) sauerkraut, drained
2 tablespoons sorghum (or dark brown sugar)
1 teaspoon caraway seeds
½ teaspoon aniseed
1 teaspoon pepper
2 tablespoons cornstarch
½ cup cold water
2 tablespoons thick steak sauce

Mix the apple juice with the can of water. Add to it the dried apricots, prunes and pears. Mix and let stand for 5 or 6 hours or until you are ready to prepare the dish.

Sauté the onion slices in margarine in a Dutch oven. Add the sliced knockwurst and the sauerkraut and stir well for a few minutes. Add the drained fruit. Mix, cover, and cook for about 30 minutes. Add the sorghum, caraway, aniseed, and pepper. Mix the cornstarch with ½ cup cold water. Stir in the steak sauce. Add this mixture to the sauerkraut mixture and stir until the sauce has thickened slightly. Boil for 2 more minutes. Serves 6.

DEEP DISH PIE WITH KRAUT AND FRANKS

      1 pound frankfurters, cut up
      2 cans sauerkraut
      1 can condensed celery (or mushroom) soup
      1 medium onion, diced
      1 teaspoon dry mustard
2–8-ounce cans ready-made biscuits
    ½ cup shredded Cheddar cheese

Mix the frankfurters, sauerkraut, soup, onion, and dry mustard together. Roll out one can of biscuit dough to cover the bottom of a deep dish. Try to arrange the frankfurters evenly through the dish. Sprinkle the top with cheddar cheese and cover with the second can of biscuit dough rolled out. Seal edges but make some openings in the top of the dough. Bake at 400° for 20 minutes. Serves 6.

(Pastry can be made from ready-made dry biscuit mix flour by following the directions given on box.)

121

HASH WITH SAUERKRAUT
AND FRANKFURTERS

½ cup milk
¼ stick butter or margarine
 4 cups cooked mashed potatoes or instant potatoes
 2 egg yolks
 1 medium onion, grated
 2 cups drained sauerkraut
 1 pound frankfurters, cut in 1-inch pieces
Salt and pepper to taste

In a saucepan heat milk with butter (or margarine).
Add mashed potatoes and beat in egg yolks. Mix in the
onion, sauerkraut, and frankfurters. Season to taste and
cook over medium heat 15 minutes or longer, mixing frequently. Can be browned over high heat for five minutes
just before serving. Serves 6–8.

122

BRAISED LAMB SHANKS WITH SAUERKRAUT

3–4 pounds (6–8 pieces) lamb shanks
Oil
  2 cups water
  1 quart sauerkraut, drained
  1 large onion, chopped
  3 tablespoons flour
  1 tablespoon sugar
Pepper to taste
Caraway seeds to taste
Curry powder to taste
 12 small potatoes, peeled

Brown the lamb shanks in a little hot oil. Remove them to a large shallow casserole and add 2 cups of water. Bake at 400° for 30 minutes. Reduce the heat to 325° and bake for 2 hours more. Mix the sauerkraut with the onion, flour, sugar, pepper, caraway seeds, and curry powder and pour the mixture over the lamb shanks. Pile the potatoes on top. Bake for another 45 minutes at 375°. Serves 6–8.

SAUERKRAUT WITH BRISKET OF BEEF

3 pound brisket of beef
1 quart sauerkraut, drained
2 medium onions, sliced
2 large potatoes, sliced
Pepper
2 tablespoons sugar
1 teaspoon caraway seeds
2 tablespoons flour

Cook beef brisket covered with water in a large saucepan for about 2 hours, or until brisket is almost tender. Change the water if it becomes too greasy. Add sauerkraut, sliced onion, sliced potatoes, pepper, sugar, and caraway. Boil for 30 minutes. Mix flour with a little water to make a paste. When brisket is tender add the flour mixture to thicken the sauce. Serves 6–8.

ROAST VENISON WITH SAUERKRAUT

5–8 pounds of venison rump
  2 quarts sauerkraut
Onion, minced
  1 clove garlic
  2 cups broth
½ cup gin or 12 juniper berries

Sear the venison roast in hot oven, 425° for 15 minutes until brown. Roast the venison with the sauerkraut placed over the entire top. Sprinkle on the minced onion and minced garlic clove and saturate the pan with broth and gin. Roast at 350° for about 2½ hours or 15 minutes to the pound.

GOOSE STUFFED WITH SAUERKRAUT

1 egg
2 onions, minced
3 cups grated potatoes
2 pounds sauerkraut, drained
2 tablespoons rendered goose fat
1 teaspoon caraway seeds
1 8-10 pound goose, cleaned
1 can concentrated orange juice
1 juice can water

Put egg and onions in a blender and blend well. Add the potatoes to the blender and pulverize well. (A hand grater can be used for the onions and potatoes.) Mix the sauerkraut together with the onion, egg, and potato mixture. Render the goose fat in a pan. Add the sauerkraut mixture and the caraway seeds and cook slowly for about 15 minutes or until it sticks together. Cool the stuffing until it can be handled easily. Stuff the goose and bake in the usual way. Mix the orange juice and water and baste the goose frequently.

DUCK WITH SAUERKRAUT, GRAPES, AND ORANGES
(Greek Version)

1 large duck, at least 5-6 pounds
½ cup flour
1 teaspoon salt
1 teaspoon pepper
1 tablespoon paprika
Duck fat
4 cups sauerkraut
1 onion, chopped
1 cup canned or sliced oranges
1 cup white grapes
1 cup white wine
1 cup broth

Have the duck cut into pieces. Dredge in flour seasoned with salt, pepper, and paprika. Brown in fat taken from inside the duck. (If not enough fat is available use cooking oil or butter.) Place sauerkraut at the bottom of a large greased casserole. Sprinkle on the chopped onion and spread the oranges and grapes evenly. Top with the duck pieces. Add the wine and broth to the browning pan. Pour this over the casserole, bake uncovered at 325° for 2 to 2½ hours or until the duck is tender. Baste the duck frequently with the pan juices.

PHEASANT WITH SAUERKRAUT

      2 quarts sauerkraut, drained
      1 stick butter
      2 cups water
      2 onions (1 minced, 1 sliced)
      1 clove garlic, minced
      1 teaspoon pepper
    12 juniper berries or 1 ounce gin
    1½ cups white wine
    1½ cups broth
      2 potatoes, grated
      ½ cup Kirsch
      2 pheasants
      ½ pound bacon
      1 pound hot sausage
      1 cup white wine
Boiled potatoes

Rinse the sauerkraut and cook it gently with the butter and water for 10 minutes. Add the chopped onion, garlic, pepper, juniper berries, white wine, broth, and potatoes and transfer to a baking dish. Bake for 1½ hours. Add the Kirsch and toss well. At the same time, roast the pheasants which have been topped with the sliced bacon. Baste frequently with the drippings. Remove the bacon for the last 10 minutes to let the birds get brown. Poach the sausage in 1 cup of white wine with the sliced onion. Simmer for about 20 minutes.

Arrange the sauerkraut on a large platter. Carve the pheasants and put the quarters or halves on the sauerkraut. Slice the sausage in rings and distribute abound the pheasant pieces. Garnish with the bacon. Place boiled potatoes around the edge of the platter. Serves 6–8.

FISH BAKED IN SAUERKRAUT

3 pounds firm fish, such as pike
Onion slices
Salt
Pepper
¼ pound bacon
2 onions, minced
3 tablespoons flour
1 cup fish stock
1 quart sauerkraut, drained
4 tablespoons butter
½ cup cream
Salt
Pepper
Paprika
1 cup bread crumbs

Boil the firm-fleshed (white) fish in water for 10 minutes with a few slices of onion, salt, and pepper. When the fish is done, drain the stock but save it for the sauce. Remove as much bone as possible. Fry the bacon in bits until crisp; add the onion and sauerkraut and sauté mixing frequently to keep from burning the kraut. Mix the flour in a cup of the fish stock. Add this to the butter in a separate saucepan, mixing thoroughly to prevent lumps. Add the cream, salt, pepper, paprika, and more fish stock until the sauce is the desired thickness.

Place a layer of sauerkraut in a casserole dish, cover with a layer of bread crumbs and a few pieces of fish. Continue the layers until all of the sauerkraut, bread crumbs, and fish are used. (Use more bread crumbs if necessary.) Top with the sauce. Dot generously with butter and bake at 375° for 40 minutes.

Variations:

Sliced boiled potatoes can be used in the casserole in place of the bread crumbs.

The fish can be dredged in flour and fried instead of boiled.

Sauerkraut Soup and Sandwiches

CORNED BEEF WITH KRAUT

Sliced pumpernickel bread
Butter
Mustard
Sliced dill pickles
Bermuda onion slices
Sliced corned beef
Sauerkraut, drained

Spread butter and mustard over bread. Add the pickles, onion, corned beef, and a layer of the drained sauerkraut. Serve while fresh.

FRANKFURTERS WITH KRAUT
(On Buns)

 1 small can sauerkraut, drained
 1 tablespoon hot mustard
 1 tablespoon chili sauce
12 frankfurters
12 long rolls
Butter

Mix drained sauerkraut with chili sauce and hot mustard. Simmer frankfurters until hot. Heat buns in oven and spread with butter. Place frankfurters on buns and top with the kraut mixture. Makes 12 rolls.

FAMED REUBEN GRILL

1 pound cooked corned beef, sliced
1 pound Swiss cheese, sliced
1 cup sauerkraut, drained
1 loaf sour rye bread
Favorite dressing

Place corned beef, a slice Swiss cheese, and some sauerkraut on a slice of bread. Spread dressing over top. Place between waffle iron grills for 5 minutes or broil open face under broiler until the sauerkraut is well heated.

HEARTY QUICK SAUERKRAUT SOUP
(Meal in One)

1 pound beef, ground coarse
2 cups sauerkraut
2 cups canned tomatoes
1 tablespoon brown sugar
1 teaspoon salt
½ teaspoon pepper
4 cups water
1 cup instant potatoes

In a large saucepan, brown the ground beef. Add the sauerkraut, tomatoes, sugar, salt, pepper, and water. Simmer for 30 minutes or more. Just before serving add the instant potatoes. Serve in soup dishes with Italian bread or rye bread. Serves 4–5.

CZECHOSLOVAKIAN SAUERKRAUT SOUP

2 pounds short ribs
2 pounds beef bones
2 tablespoons salt
1 clove garlic
1 tablespoon pepper
1 teaspoon thyme
2 cups canned tomatoes
½ cup sugar
3 cups shredded cabbage
3 cups sauerkraut, drained
4 cups potatoes, peeled and cut up
2 cups peeled and sliced carrots
2 cups quartered onions
Sour cream

Using a very large kettle brown the short ribs on all sides. Add the beef bones to the kettle and add water to cover all. Bring to a boil and simmer for about 3 hours. Add the salt, garlic, pepper, thyme, tomatoes, and sugar and simmer for another half hour. Add the cabbage, sauerkraut, potatoes, carrots, and onions. Boil for another 35 minutes. If necessary, add water to keep the soup from getting too heavy. This is a one-dish meal. Serve bread on the side. The soup can be garnished with sour cream, if desired. Serves 6–8.

ALSATIAN SAUERKRAUT SOUP

4–5 slices bacon, diced
  2 cups sauerkraut
  2 onions, diced
  1 apple, diced
  4 tablespoons flour
  ½ tablespoon caraway seed
  2 quarts beef stock
  ¼ cup honey
Salt
Pepper
  ½ cup white wine
Croutons

Fry diced bacon until crisp. Toss in sauerkraut, onion, and apple and pan-fry for about 5 minutes. Add the other seasonings plus the beef stock. If you have no beef stock you can use water and bouillon, adding the bouillon until you have reached your desired taste. Remember the sauerkraut enhances the flavor of bouillon. If bouillon is used, be cautious with the salt. Add wine just before serving. Top with croutons. Croutons can be made at home by dicing bread and pan-frying quickly in a bit of butter or bacon drippings. Serves 6–8.

HEARTY SAUERKRAUT SOUP

3–4 pounds short ribs of beef, shin beef, or knucklebones
Oil
   1 cup chopped carrots
   1 cup sliced onions
   1 clove garlic
½ teaspoon thyme
   1 bay leaf
   1 tablespoon salt
   1 teaspoon pepper
   1 can (2 cups) tomatoes
   4 cups shredded cabbage
   3 cup drained sauerkraut
   2 cups mashed potatoes (made from instant potatoes)
½ cup lemon juice
   2 tablespoons sugar
   2 cups sour cream

Brown the short ribs in a little oil in a hot skillet. Put the ribs into a large kettle with a cover. Add water to cover the meat. Add the carrots, onions, garlic, thyme, and bay leaf. Season with salt and pepper and simmer for 3 to 4 hours. Remove the bones from the soup, strip the meat, and return the meat to the pot. Stir in the tomatoes, cabbage, and sauerkraut. Boil for another 30 minutes. Mix in the mashed potatoes, lemon juice, and sugar. Serve in soup bowls, topped with sour cream with sour rye bread and butter on the side. Serves 6 or more.

Sauerkraut Salads

SUMMER SAUERKRAUT SALAD

2 cups sauerkraut
Peach halves
Apricot halves
White grapes, seedless
Dark grapes, halved and seeded
Strawberries
Blueberries
Cottage cheese

Dressing:
1 tablespoon honey
½ cup mayonnaise
½ cup syrup from fruit
½ teaspoon cinnamon

Wash sauerkraut well. Scoop cottage cheese onto the peach halves. Surround each peach half with a circle of sauerkraut and garnish with other fruits. Mix dressing thoroughly. Dribble over salad.

SAUERKRAUT SALAD WITH WHITE GRAPES

4 cups sauerkraut
1 cup white grapes
1 tablespoon minced scallions
1 apple diced

Sauce:
2 tablespoons vinegar
2 tablespoons oil or bacon fat
2 tablespoons brown sugar

Mix all solid ingredients in bowl. Mix the sauce separately and toss lightly with the sauerkraut mixture. Will keep well. Serves 8–10.

SAUERKRAUT AND APPLE SALAD

Dressing:
½ cup sour cream
½ tablespoon parsley flakes
2 tablespoons honey
¼ teaspoon caraway seeds
⅛ teaspoon aniseed
½ cup mayonnaise

Salad:
1 cup diced apples
2 cups sauerkraut
Lettuce leaves

Make dressing first by mixing above ingredients. Chop apples and mix with the sauerkraut. Pour dressing over immediately and place on bed of lettuce leaves. Serves 4–6.

SAUERKRAUT SALAD

2–3 cups drained sauerkraut
1 cup shredded carrots
1 medium onion, chopped
½ cup green pepper, sliced fine
½ cup celery, sliced fine
½ cup sugar
¼ cup olive oil

Wash the sauerkraut and drain off all moisture. Add the carrots, onions, green pepper, and celery. Mix the oil with sugar and pour over the vegetables. Let stand at least 3 to 4 hours before serving. Will keep at least a week in refrigeration. Serves 6–8.

SWEET SAUERKRAUT SALAD

1 can sauerkraut (8 ounces)
2 tablespoons honey
2 tablespoons tiny marshmallows
2 tablespoons raisins
2 tablespoons mayonnaise
¼ teaspoon aniseed
½ cup drained crushed pineapple

Rinse sauerkraut under running water. Squeeze well. Combine all ingredients. Allow to stand 4 to 6 hours. Serves 8.

VEGETABLE SAUERKRAUT SALAD

2 cups sauerkraut, drained
1 medium cucumber, sliced
1 medium onion, sliced fine
2 raw apples, diced
½ cup honey
¼ cup olive oil
½ cup sour cream

Mix the drained sauerkraut with the cucumber, onion, and apple. Combine the honey, olive oil, and sour cream. Mix with the vegetables. Refrigerate 1 hour or more before serving. Spices such as caraway, aniseed, or celery seed can be added to the dressing. Serves 6–8.

SAUERKRAUT RELISH

3–4 cups sauerkraut
1 cup minced celery
1 cup sugar
2 ounces pimiento
1 medium onion, diced
1 green pepper, minced fine
1 teaspoon salt
½ teaspoon pepper
½ cup tarragon vinegar
1 green tomato

Drain the sauerkraut and wash one time only. Drain well. Mix all ingredients together. Refrigerate in a covered bowl for 1 day. Keeps well for over a week.

144

Desserts and Appetizers

SAUERKRAUT BALLS

1 cup ground ham
1 cup ground fresh pork
1 cup ground beef
1 medium onion, chopped
2 cups milk
1 teaspoon dry mustard
1 teaspoon salt
2 cups flour
1 can sauerkraut, drained and chopped fine
Beaten egg
Bread crumbs
Frying oil

Pan fry the meats and onion together until browned. Stir in the milk, mustard, salt, and 1 cup of the flour. Cook together until fluffy. Cool. When cool add the sauerkraut and mix thoroughly. Chill in the refrigerator for 2 hours. Shape into balls about the size of walnuts. Roll first in the remaining flour, then in the beaten egg, and then in the bread crumbs. Fry in hot fat (375°) until well browned. Drain on paper towels and serve hot. These are good for a cocktail party and can be frozen. Makes 36–40 **balls.**

SAUERKRAUT JUICE COCKTAIL

2 cups sauerkraut juice
1 tablespoon lemon
¼ teaspoon caraway seed
1 cup cider
1 tablespoon honey

Combine all ingredients and let stand in the refrigerator for 4 hours. Serve cold in cocktail glasses. Serves 6–8.

QUICK CABBAGE STRUDEL
(Sauerkraut)

1 stick butter or margerine
1 onion, minced fine
1 medium head cabbage, shredded very fine
2 cups brown sugar
½ teaspoon salt
1 teaspoon cinnamon
1 cup dark raisins
1 cup golden raisins
1 package prepared flaky pastry

Melt butter or margarine in skillet and sauté onion until soft. Add cabbage and toss; cook until tender, about 10 minutes. Add sugar, salt, cinnamon, and raisins and mix well. Sauté for another 5 minutes. Roll out flaky pastry into circles. Place ¼ cup of cabbage mixture on each circle and fold over. Place edges together and seal with a little water if necessary. Put on greased baking dish. Brush with butter. Bake at 350° for 15 to 20 minutes or until golden brown. (Drained sauerkraut may be substituted for cabbage.)

KRAUT CHOCOLATE CAKE

⅔ cup softened margarine
1½ cups sugar
3 eggs
2¼ cups all-purpose flour
½ cup cocoa
1 teaspoon soda
1½ teaspoons baking powder
½ teaspoon salt
1 cup water
1 teaspoon vanilla extract
¾ cup sauerkraut, rinsed, drained, and chopped fine

Cream margarine and sugar until fluffy. Add one egg at a time and beat well. Combine the dry ingredients, add to the creamed mixture, alternating with the water. Add vanilla and stir in the kraut. Use 2 8-inch greased cake pans and bake at 350° for 35 minutes, or until cakes test done. Cool on rack. Frost when cool.

Index

154